THE VALUE OF RESPECT

The Story of Abraham Lincoln

VALUE COMMUNICATION
PUBLISHERS
LA JOLLA, CALIFORNI

THE
VALUE
OF
RESPECT

ILLUSTRATED BY Pileggi

The Story of
Abraham Lincoln

BY ANN DONEGAN JOHNSON

The Value of Respect is part of the ValueTales series.

The Value of Respect text copyright © 1977 by Ann Donegan Johnson. Illustrations copyright © 1977 by Value Communications, Inc.

First Edition
Manufactured in the United States of America
For information write to: ValueTales, P.O. Box 1012
La Jolla, CA 92038

Library of Congress Cataloging in Publication Data

Johnson, Ann Donegan.
    The value of respect.

    (ValueTales)
    SUMMARY: A brief biography of Abraham Lincoln emphasizing the importance of respect in his life.
       1.   Lincoln, Abraham, Pres. U.S., 1809–1865—Juvenile literature.   2.   Presidents—United States—Biography—Juvenile literature.   3.   Respect—Juvenile literature.
[1.   Lincoln, Abraham, Pres. U.S., 1809–1865.
2.   Presidents.   3.   Respect]   I.   Title.
E457.905.J63   973.7'092'4   [B]   [92]   77-12455

ISBN 0-916392-14-7

To Dr. Joseph Pennario whose
devotion to children I respect.

This tale is about the respected Abraham
Lincoln. The story that follows is largely based
on events in his early life. More historical facts
about Abraham Lincoln can be found on page 63.

Once upon a time...

not so very long ago, there lived a man named Abraham Lincoln. He was President of the United States.

People listened to Lincoln when he spoke. When he went out to walk, they crowded around him. Almost everyone loved him and admired him. And even those who didn't love him, respected him very much.

One day, after Abe Lincoln and his son Tad had been out walking, Tad thought about the people he had seen crowding around his father.

"You know, Father," said Tad, "I hope that some day people will respect me the way they respect you."

"They will if you have respect for them," said Abe. "We all usually get back what we give, you know. And you can respect people for many different reasons. Of course you respect them first of all because they're human beings."

Later, Abe sat looking out of a window, watching the squirrels scamper about on the White House Lawn. He thought about what Tad had said.

"What we learn when we're children is so important," he told himself. "It makes all the difference when we grow up and go out into the world."

Then Abe's mind went back to the days when he was a child himself.

He remembered his mother and father, and his sister Sarah, who was two years older. He remembered the one-room log cabin on the farm deep in the wilderness of Kentucky where they all lived together. There wasn't much furniture in the cabin, for Abe's family had almost no money. The soil on their farm was not good. So Abe's father had to spend long, hard hours trying to make his crops grow.

Abe's mother worked hard, too, looking after her husband and the children. She made all the clothes for the family. Abe grew so fast that she could hardly keep up with him.

"Abraham," she would say, "You grow out of everything. What am I going to *do* with you?"

She tried to sound stern and severe when she said this, but she was really very pleased. She knew that Abe was a strong, healthy boy, happy to play in the woods and help his father with the chores.

Sometimes, when the sun was warm and the birds were singing, Mrs. Lincoln took Abe and Sarah to play in the stream near their farm.

"We're lucky to have the beautiful trees around us," she told them. "And lucky to have the clear stream to bathe in and the fresh air to breathe."

"I guess we are," said Abe, "and it's a good thing some things are free. We could not buy them if they weren't. We're too poor."

"Being poor is nothing to be ashamed of," said his mother. "As long as you are honest, and you respect other people, they will respect you no matter how poor you are!"

Abe's neighbors did not live close by. When Abe wanted to play with his friends, he would have to walk a long distance. Sometimes he went off to play with his friend Austin. And sometimes he got into trouble.

One day he was crossing a creek, using a fallen log as a footbridge. But it had been raining and the log was slippery. Abe's legs went flying out from under him. Abe yelled. Then he landed in the creek with a huge SPLASH!!

Luckily, Austin saw Abe fall. He ran toward the creek as fast as his legs would carry him.

"Hang on, Abe!" he cried. "I'll have you out in a jiffy!"

He found a long pole and held it toward Abe. Abe grabbed the end of the pole, and Austin pulled him to safety.

"Do you always go swimming in your clothes, Abe?" asked Austin, as Abe crawled out of the creek.

"Aw stop kidding," replied Abe.

Abe was cold and dripping, but he had to laugh in spite of himself.

Abe might laugh, but his mother knew that there was more to life than just running through the woods.

"I'm sending you to school," she said to Abe one day. "It's high time you learned to read and write."

This didn't sound like fun to Abe. "Oh, Mother," he said, "hardly anybody around here goes to school."

"I know," answered his mother, "but education is very important. No one will ever listen to you or respect you if you can't even read and write."

So both Sarah and Abe went off to school. And they had to hike for two miles on a dirt road to get there.

"My feet hurt!" complained poor Sarah. "I sure hope this is going to be worth it!"

"Me too," said Abe.

They soon learned to make the time pass quickly on the way to school and home again. Abe and Sarah talked about the things they learned at school.

Actually, they didn't learn many of the things that children learn in school today. They weren't very comfortable while they were learning, either. There was only a single classroom in the log schoolhouse. And the older children sat on wooden benches right alongside the younger ones. There were no windows in the school and the children had no books to read.

How did they learn? They learned by listening to the teacher and repeating what she said.

"Now children," she would say, "repeat after me: C-A-T spells cat."

The children repeated the word over and over again. After a while, they knew how to spell cat. Soon Abe and Sarah could spell quite a few words.

When Abe and Sarah came home from school they always told their mother about the things they had learned. Then they did their chores. And they did them cheerfully. The children liked to help their mother because they respected her. She was a kind person who took very good care of her family.

Abe and Sarah were happy enough in Kentucky, but
Mr. Lincoln was not. He was tired of trying to grow
enough food for his family in the poor soil of his farm.

"Children," he said one night, "we are going to move to
Indiana. Life should be easier there. The soil is better so
we can grow bigger crops."

Abe was a bit upset when he heard this. "Do you mean
I have to leave all my friends?" he asked.

"Don't worry," said his mother. "You'll make lots of
new friends when we get to Indiana."

Abe knew this was probably true, but he still felt lonely.

Now in those days, the country was very different from the way it is today. There were no cars or busses, and no smooth roads to travel on. So the trip to Indiana was a great adventure. The Lincoln family began their journey by horseback. Then they borrowed a wagon and piled all their belongings on it. As they traveled along, the roads began to get narrower and narrower.

"Are we nearly there?" asked Abe, when they finally had to chop down bushes in order to move the wagon.

"Just about," said Mr. Lincoln. And indeed, they soon reached a nice clearing. Mr. Lincoln decided that they had come to the end of their journey. At last they had found a good place to build a cabin.

They wanted to get a shelter up quickly so they would be protected. Everyone pitched in to help. Abe was working as hard as he could when he imagined he saw a squirrel hop onto a tree stump.

"Hi, Abe," said the squirrel. "No need to be lonely around here. You and I can be friends."

Abe was pretending. He laughed because he realized that the squirrel was just a little creature he had made up to keep from feeling sad about the friends he had left behind in Kentucky.

When the cabin was finished, Abe invited his little make-believe friend, the talking squirrel, to move in with him.

The cabin was called a half-faced camp because it had only three sides. The open side was where the Lincolns built their fires and cooked their meals.

"Father says we're going to build a bigger, nicer cabin soon," said Abe, as he and the squirrel snuggled down on his bed of dried leaves.

The next year the Lincolns did build a better cabin. But before they had lived in it long, a great sadness came to them. Mrs. Lincoln died of a sickness that could not be cured in those days.

Abe and Sarah were terribly lonely. Mr. Lincoln did his best to cheer them. "Your mother would not want us to sit around being sad all the time," he told them. "She'd want us to keep busy and try to be happy."

Abe and Sarah knew their father was right. They did try to keep busy. And there was a lot to do.

Water had to be brought up from the nearby spring. Clothes had to be scrubbed in a big wooden tub. Food had to be cooked in the fireplace, and bread had to be baked in the outdoor oven. The dirt floor had to be swept with a broom made of twigs.

Abe and Sarah did their best, but the work never seemed to get finished. Sometimes, long after the sun had set they were still busy gathering wood for the fire.

Abe and Sarah worked hard and tried to be brave, even though they missed their mother very much. Mr. Lincoln respected them for trying. But he could see how terribly lonely they were.

"Children," said Mr. Lincoln one day, "I am going away for a little while. When I return, I might have a surprise for you."

What do you think the surprise could be?

Mr. Lincoln returned home with his surprise in a few weeks. He had a new wife, whose name was Sarah. Sarah was a widow who Mr. Lincoln had known for a long time. They also had Sarah's two daughters, Sarah and Matilda, and her son, John. Sarah and Abe could not believe their eyes.

"What dear children," said their new stepmother as she reached out her arms to give Abe and Sarah a big hug. "We are all going to be such a nice big happy family."

"I'm getting mixed up!" said Abe's little friend the squirrel. "There are so many people named Sarah around here."

Abe looked at the wagon that had carried his new family to the farm. He saw that it was filled with wonderful things. There were tables and chairs and pots and pans, and the softest feather mattresses you could possibly imagine.

31

The new Mrs. Lincoln hurried excitedly into the cabin that was to be her new home. She looked at the dust and at the beds that were made out of leaves. She frowned at the broken furniture. "We're going to get rid of all this," she said in a cheery way. "We're going to get rid of the loneliness, too. From now on we'll have only bright, happy things around here!"

That night, Abe slept in a real bed for the first time. He nestled down in a feather mattress with his head on a soft pillow, and he couldn't believe that anything could feel so warm and cozy.

"I feel sorry for people who do not have a real bed to sleep in," Abe said to his little friend.

The squirrel snuggled down beside him. "I agree," he said, in a sleepy little voice. "I'm warm as toast."

Time passed joyfully now, and Abe grew older and taller and stronger. He helped his father more and more. He plowed and planted, and he chopped down trees with his double-edged ax.

"Wow," said the other boys. "Just look at Abe Lincoln! He's the biggest boy around here. Don't ever get into a fight with him. He could probably throw you right over a fence!"

If Abe heard the others talk, he didn't pay any attention.
He was much too busy to be thinking of fights.

But he was never too busy to show his stepmother that he loved her. One day he came in from the fields, swept her off her feet and lifted her into the air.

"Abe Lincoln, you put me down right now," she said. "All that heavy work you do may make your body grow, but reading and learning is just as important. They make your mind grow. I'm going to try to get you lots of books so you can read and learn things."

36

Abe soon found that he really enjoyed reading. He sat by the fire at night when the others were asleep, and he read every book he could find. He didn't have paper to write on, so he used a wooden shovel. He wrote on it with a bit of charcoal.

"Golly, there's a lot to learn," said the squirrel.

"You bet there is," agreed Abe. "I guess I'll never know it all."

Sometimes Abe just couldn't put down his books. Once in a while he tried to read and do chores at the same time.

"I can't believe it," said the little squirrel. "You may learn lots of great things from those books, but you've forgotten how to plow a straight line."

Abe laughed when his make-believe friend scolded him, and he tried to pay more attention to his work.

As he grew older, Abe didn't always have time to chat with the squirrel. He wanted to be with people. He liked to listen to them and find out what they thought. He liked to tell them about the things he read, and he made up jokes that set them all laughing.

"I like to talk with Abe Lincoln," said one man in the village. "I feel that he really respects me, and he wants to hear what I have to say."

"I like the way he explains things," said another man. "He makes things seem so simple."

One evening, a wealthy farmer named James Gentry came to Abe. "Abe, you're an honest man and a strong one," he said. "Would you be willing to take my goods down to New Orleans on a flatboat?"

"Yes sir, Mr. Gentry," replied Abe.

Abe had never been to a big city like New Orleans. He was terribly excited when he looked at Mr. Gentry's map. "It's a long way," he said. "A thousand miles!"

"You won't have to go alone, Abe," said Mr. Gentry. "My son Allen will go with you."

Of course Abe wanted to go. Mr. Gentry watched as he and Allen loaded the flatboat. It was a sturdy craft, with a little shelter on the deck, two sets of oars, and a steering pole.

"It will be a dangerous trip," warned Mr. Gentry. There are strong currents in the river, and bandits might try to attack you. You'll have to be careful, and you'll need all the strength you have."

41

When the boat was loaded with its cargo of apples, pork, and potatoes, Abe and Allen guided it down the Ohio River and into the great Mississippi.

Suddenly Abe knew why Allen's father had said he would need all his strength. Strong currents caught the flatboat and sent it spinning and speeding down the stream. It was all Abe could do to steer clear of the big rocks that seemed to jump up at them.

"Easy there, Abe!" cried the squirrel. "Can't we go a little slower? I can't stay on my feet!"

When they stopped for the night, Abe and Allen tied
the flatboat to a tree on the riverbank. Then they settled
down to rest until morning.

"That was a rough day," said the squirrel one evening.
"I'm worn out."

"Tomorrow could be just as bad," warned Abe.

But that same night, a new danger threatened them.
What do you think it was?

River bandits!

As darkness fell, seven of these dangerous thieves crept out from behind the trees.

"There's a rich cargo on that flatboat," said one of the bandits, "and there are only two men to protect it. Come on! They won't give us much trouble!"

The bandits rushed aboard the boat. And what do you suppose happened then?

Abe jumped up. He grabbed a stout stick and he swung it with all the strength he had.

The river bandits shouted and yelled. They tried to cover their heads with their arms.

"That will teach you to try to rob us," roared Abe.

"Next time, have a little respect!" cried the squirrel.

One by one the bandits jumped out of the flatboat and ran away into the night. Abe and Allen jumped to the shore and chased after them, but the thieves disappeared into the woods like frightened shadows.

"Maybe they'll come back," said the squirrel, "but it wouldn't surprise me if they simply gave up being bandits."

"Being a bandit doesn't pay when Abe Lincoln's around," said the squirrel.

Allen looked at Abe with a new respect. "You're as strong as half a dozen men," he said.

"Maybe," said Abe. "But that didn't stop me from getting a whack on the head." Abe took out his handkerchief and bandaged the cut over his eye.

Abe and Allen didn't meet any more bandits on the river. They reached New Orleans safely and unloaded their cargo. Then they set out to explore the city.

Abe couldn't believe his eyes. He had never seen such elegant buildings. He had never seen so many different kinds of people. He had never heard the kind of music being played on the streets. And wherever he went, delicious smells floated on the air.

HOTEL

FRESH
SHRIMP

"This is more exciting than I ever imagined!" said Abe to Allen.

But suddenly Abe and Allen turned a corner and came upon a big square. There they saw something that Abe would never forget.

Do you know what it was?

It was a slave market!

Abe saw black men and women and children chained together. They were being sold just as if they were horses, sheep or cows.

Of course Abe had heard about slavery, but he had never before seen people treated as if they were animals.

"Allen, those black people are human beings, too," said Abe. "They deserve respect, just like everyone else."

At that time, it was not unusual to sell black people in slave markets. They had no rights at all. And they had to do whatever their masters told them to.

"Someday," said Abe Lincoln, "I'm going to try to put a stop to things like this."

Allen looked at Abe, and he believed it. When Abe Lincoln said something, he meant it.

Abe returned home, but he could not forget what he had seen in the slave market. He told his friends about the chains and about how husbands were separated from their wives. "And children are taken away from their parents and sold to new masters," said Abe. "The black people have feelings, just as we do. How can anyone treat a human being that way, with no respect?"

No one could answer Abe's question, but almost everyone Abe talked to agreed that slavery was a terrible thing.

Abe didn't forget the black people, or any other people who weren't treated fairly. "Soon I'll be on my own," he said to his friend the squirrel. "I'll go out into the world and talk with people. I'd like to know what they really need, and how I can help them."

"That's great!" said the squirrel. "And of course you can help them. You respect people, no matter who they are. And so almost everyone respects you."

When it was time for Abe to leave home and strike out on his own, he put his few belongings into a handkerchief and tied it to a stick. Then he said goodbye to his family and his friends.

"I've learned so much from all of you," he said. "I'll never forget you."

"We won't forget you, either," said his little friend the squirrel. He waved goodbye as Abe headed out into the world to begin a new life.

57

First Abe headed for Salem, Illinois. He got a job tending store, and at night he studied law books so he could become a lawyer.

The people who knew him were sure that Abe would be a great lawyer. "Abe Lincoln cares about people and he is honest," they said.

Abe met many people when he became a lawyer. They respected him because he listened to them. They knew he cared. After a while, Abe was elected to represent them in the state legislature.

Now Abe was really busy, fighting for the rights of other people. Later, he got married, and had children of his own.

59

There was another election for Abe. This time he represented the people in the Congress of the United States. While he was in Washington, he showed that he would treat everyone with respect.

Later, when a man named Douglas spoke out in favor of slavery, Abe argued against him. He told the people how wrong it was to have slaves.

People all over the country now knew of Abe Lincoln.

By this time there was trouble in the country. The southern states said they would form their own country if the northerners would not let them keep their slaves. Could Abe save the country from being divided? The people thought he could. They elected him President.

A long war, called the Civil War, started shortly after he became President. During this war, Abe wrote a famous paper called the Emancipation Proclamation which freed all the slaves in the United States. Abe Lincoln did save the country from being divided. And he gained the respect of people everywhere, which lasts until this day.

Abraham Lincoln realized that the things he learned in his childhood brought happiness to him throughout his life. Respect for others and being respected by them made Abe a happy person. If happiness is important to you, maybe you might want to bring respect into your life, too.

The End

Abraham Lincoln was born on February 12, 1809 in a dirt-floored log cabin in the frontier wilderness of central Kentucky. He lived with his father, Thomas, a farmer and carpenter, his mother, Nancy, and his older sister, Sarah. The Lincoln family was poor. Seeking a better life, they moved several times when Abe was young. First, they moved to another location in Kentucky, then to Indiana and, finally, to Illinois. When Abe was nine his mother died of a disease known as milk sickness.

The Lincoln home was filled with loneliness until Abe's father remarried. Abe's new stepmother, Sarah Johnson, and her three children brought happiness to the Lincoln cabin. It was Abe's step-mother who stimulated his interest in learning and reading. His knowledge and natural sense of humor resulted in Abe becoming a popular speaker.

Abe grew very strong and was uncommonly tall (six feet, four inches) for his time. At age nineteen he was asked to take cargo one thousand miles down river to New Orleans on a flat boat. It was because of his honesty and his incredible strength that he was chosen to make the perilous journey.

Abe left home at age twenty-one and went to New Salem, Illinois, a community of log cabins near the state capital of Springfield. He took a job as a clerk in a store and began to study law at night. He later bought a grocery store. The store failed but Abe voluntarily paid off all its debts, an act for which he was nicknamed "Honest Abe." By now he had taken an interest in politics.

In 1834, he was elected to the Illinois state legislature where he served four consecutive two-year terms. In 1836, he received his license to practice law and eventually gained a reputation as an able and effective lawyer.

In 1842, he married Mary Todd. They had four sons, Robert, Edward, William and Thomas (Tad).

Abe's first exposure to national politics came when he was elected to the U.S. House of Representatives in 1846. He served only one term. He returned to his law practice in Springfield and, for awhile, lost interest in politics.

In 1855, with slavery now a national political issue, Abe once again became interested in politics. Abe spoke out against slavery but was defeated in a bid for a U.S. Senate seat. In 1858, he again tried for a seat in the Senate, against the

ABRAHAM LINCOLN
1809–1865

incumbent Steven A. Douglas. Abe, in a series of seven debates with Douglas, condemned slavery "as a moral, social and political evil." Douglas won the election but the debates gained Abe a national reputation.

Abe's reputation resulted in his nomination for President in 1860 by the anti-slavery Republican Party. On November 6 of that year he was elected President. Before he could take office, seven states, led by South Carolina, seceded from the Union. The Civil War began when troops from the southern states fired on Fort Sumter in Charleston harbor, South Carolina in April, 1861. The war raged for almost exactly four years.

On September 22, 1862, Abe issued his Emancipation Proclamation which declared that all slaves in the Confederate states were free. This action led to the 13th Amendment to the Constitution which abolished slavery in all parts of the United States.

Abe was easily re-elected in 1864 to a second term as President. The Civil War was drawing to a close. On April 9, 1865, General Robert E. Lee surrendered the Confederate forces to General Ulysses S. Grant. Five days later, on April 14, 1865, Abe was assassinated while attending a play at Ford's Theater in Washington, D.C. by John Wilkes Booth, an actor and fanatical supporter of the Confederacy.

63

The ValueTale Series

THE VALUE OF BELIEVING IN YOURSELF — The Story of Louis Pasteur
THE VALUE OF DETERMINATION — The Story of Helen Keller
THE VALUE OF PATIENCE — The Story of the Wright Brothers
THE VALUE OF KINDNESS — The Story of Elizabeth Fry
THE VALUE OF HUMOR — The Story of Will Rogers
THE VALUE OF TRUTH AND TRUST — The Story of Cochise
THE VALUE OF CARING — The Story of Eleanor Roosevelt
THE VALUE OF COURAGE — The Story of Jackie Robinson
THE VALUE OF CURIOSITY — The Story of Christopher Columbus
THE VALUE OF RESPECT — The Story of Abraham Lincoln
THE VALUE OF IMAGINATION — The Story of Charles Dickens
THE VALUE OF FAIRNESS — The Story of Nellie Bly
THE VALUE OF SAVING — The Story of Benjamin Franklin
THE VALUE OF LEARNING — The Story of Marie Curie
THE VALUE OF SHARING — The Story of the Mayo Brothers
THE VALUE OF RESPONSIBILITY — The Story of Ralph Bunche
THE VALUE OF HONESTY — The Story of Confucius
THE VALUE OF GIVING — The Story of Ludwig van Beethoven
THE VALUE OF UNDERSTANDING — The Story of Margaret Mead
THE VALUE OF LOVE — The Story of Johnny Appleseed
THE VALUE OF FORESIGHT — The Story of Thomas Jefferson
THE VALUE OF HELPING — The Story of Harriet Tubman
THE VALUE OF DEDICATION — The Story of Albert Schweitzer
THE VALUE OF FRIENDSHIP — The Story of Jane Addams
THE VALUE OF FANTASY — The Story of Hans Christian Andersen
THE VALUE OF ADVENTURE — The Story of Sacagawea
THE VALUE OF CREATIVITY — The Story of Thomas Edison

Great Gift Idea!

The Value Tales Tote Bag! Designed exclusively for our Program, this sturdy vinyl tote bag is just the right size for favorite Value Tales books, and would make a perfect gift for any youngster in your life. The colorful tote, featuring the whimsical Dr. Values, can be yours for just $2.00, which *includes* shipping and handling! (New York and Connecticut residents must add sales tax.)

To order, simply send your name and complete address — remember to include your zip code — to the address below. Indicate the number of tote bags you wish us to send . . . they make delightful gifts! Allow 3 to 4 weeks for delivery.

 Grolier Enterprises Corp.

Dept. ZZ
SHERMAN TURNPIKE
DANBURY, CONNECTICUT 06816